Latin Styles
For
Guitar

by Brian Chambouleyron

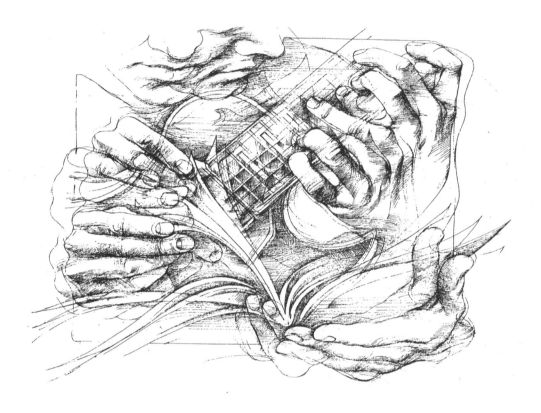

Photos: Miguel Mitlag and Brian Jait

The author wishes to acknowledge the valuable contributions of:
Luciana Gandulfo, Fernando Beckerman, Javier Cifre,
Ivan Chambouleyron, Darío Libertella and Jorge Polanuer

The following people participated in the recording:
Brian Chambouleyron: guitars, charango and keyboards
Fernando "Lechuga" Beckerman: percussion
lechu@presidentechamuyo.com.ar

All the songs are composed, arranged and produced by Brian Chambouleyron.
CD Recorded at the "Cuerda al Aire" studio, Buenos Aires, Argentina
musiclases@yahoo.com,

ISBN-13: 978-1-57424-221-8
ISBN-10:1-57424-221-0

Contents and CD Track List

Themes (guitar and accompaniment) are recorded on CD tracks 1 to 12
CD tracks 14 to 25 are accompaniment without the lead guitar (Play-a-long.)
CD track 13 is the guitar tuning notes.

Preface

The arrival of the Spanish and Portuguese conquistadors to America started an original process of culture intermixing that remains up to the present day. The process includes several components. First, the racial mixing between conquerors and the native people that prevailed for a very long time. Second, and certainly no less important than the first, was the arrival to the Americas a large contingent of African slaves. Finally, the arrival of a large number of European immigrants, particularly in the second half of the 19th and the beginning of the 20th century.

From these cultural exchanges a vast diversity of rich musical styles developed. The beauty and variety of the many musical styles of the region have fascinated me since my early student days. The twelve especially composed tunes in this book address some of the different, original styles characteristic of the Latin American people. In them, I have carefully respected the particularities that contribute to the unique beauty and richness of the musical style of the different countries.

For each piece I have suggested fingering based on the economy of movements. The numbers by the notes indicate the finger with which that note should be played, the encircled number refers to the string. There can be other ways of fingering which might be more practical for you; that being the case, feel free to modify it accordingly. There's a way to play for every instrumentalist! The pieces present different degrees of complexity; therefore, they could also make an excellent complement in learning how to play the guitar.

I hope you find this approach useful and you feel like filling yourselves with Latin styles

Enjoy it!

Brian

Brian Chambouleyron

Brian Chambouleyron became a musician studying several disciplines (guitar, singing, composition, musical analysis, arrangements and orchestration). Always fascinated with popular music, he traveled to different Latin American countries to learn their traditions. He began his professional activity as a music teacher in 1990. Teaching led to the creation of children's shows. As a composer of popular songs, he participated in the Buenos Aires' Young Artists biennial exhibition. In 1993 he went on his first professional tour to Europe, traveling all over France and Switzerland for two months and performing as both soloist and together with other musical bands. He also gave courses on Argentine popular music. From then on, his activities in European countries became regular.

In 1996 he was in charge of the musical direction of the successful show "Recuerdos son recuerdos" (which received 5 ACE awards nominations). Brian Chambouleyron was nominated for 'male revelation'. (CD Recuerdos son recuerdos – La Trastienda Records). In 1998 he participated in the show Glorias Porteñas (1998 ACE award) together with Soledad Villamil, which was given an excellent reception by the critics and the public. The show toured continuously throughout Argentina, Latin America and Europe for two years, and participated in prestigious international festivals (CD Glorias Porteñas vol. I and II – Epsa Music).

The Department of Culture of Buenos Aires City gave Brian Chambouleyron the 1999 Trinidad Guevara award for 'male revelation of the year'. In 2000 he created the show: "Patio de Tango" with Esteban Morgado, which also had a wonderful reception at a national level, and he started an extended international tour (Paris, Rome, Madrid, Barcelona, etc). (CD Patio de Tango – BAM records, Department of Culture).

With his last show, Tangos, Valses and Milongas, he has performed in several cultural events and toured abroad, being highly acclaimed by audiences and critics. Brian has also composed the music for several theater plays: "La firecilla domada", 2004; "Pequeña historia del tango", 2002; "Granadina", 2003; ect. In 2004 he recorded and arranged the CD "Chambouleyron sings Gardel", a selection of the finest compositions by Gardel. (Random records, Buenos Aires). In 2005 recorded and arranged the CD "Voice and Guitar", Twenty traditional Tango and Argentinean popular music pieces, (Random Records, Buenos Aires). In 2006 Centerstream published Brian's Argentina and Latin America compositions (with others) in the book/CD package "Tango for Guitar".

Brian Chambouleyron can be reached at:

Baldomero F. Moreno 1714 10° 111
(1406) Buenos Aires - Argentina
e-mail: brianch@infovia.com.ar
       musicacriolla@hotmail.com
web site : www.brianchambouleyron.com.ar

Bolero from México

Written by Brian Chambouleyron

8

Chorinho from Brazil

Written by Brian Chambouleyron

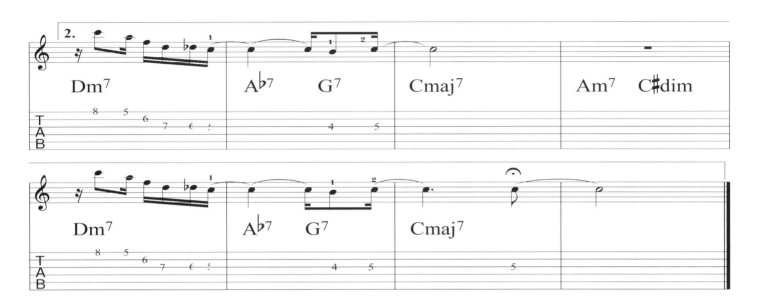

Canción from México

Written by Brian Chambouleyron

Joropo from Venezuela

Written by Brian Chambouleyron

14

Guarania from Paraguay

Dedicated to Luciana Gandulfo   Written by Brian Chambouleyron

21

Huayno from Bolivia

Written by Brian Chambouleyron

Chamarrita from Uruguay

Written by Brian Chambouleyron

27

Samba from Brazil

Written by Brian Chambouleyron

Tango from Argentina

Written by Brian Chambouleyron

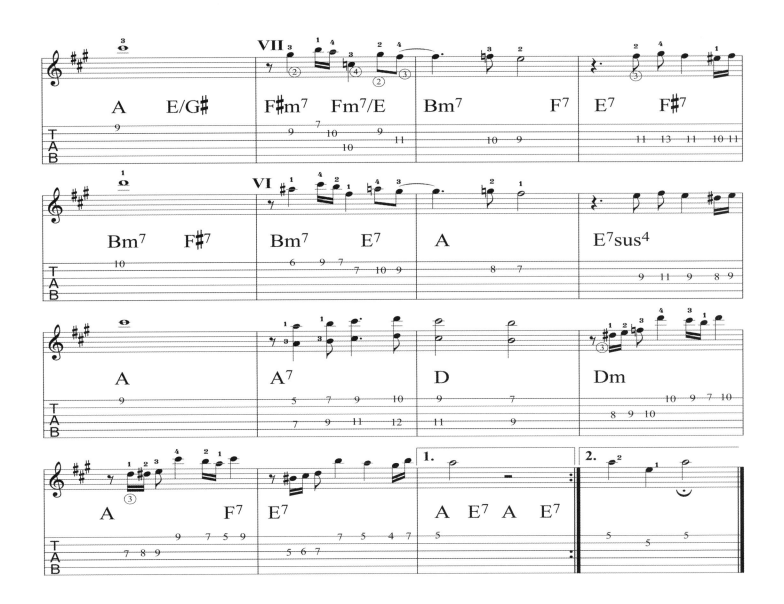

Murga-Candombe from Argentina and Uruguay

Written by Brian Chambouleyron

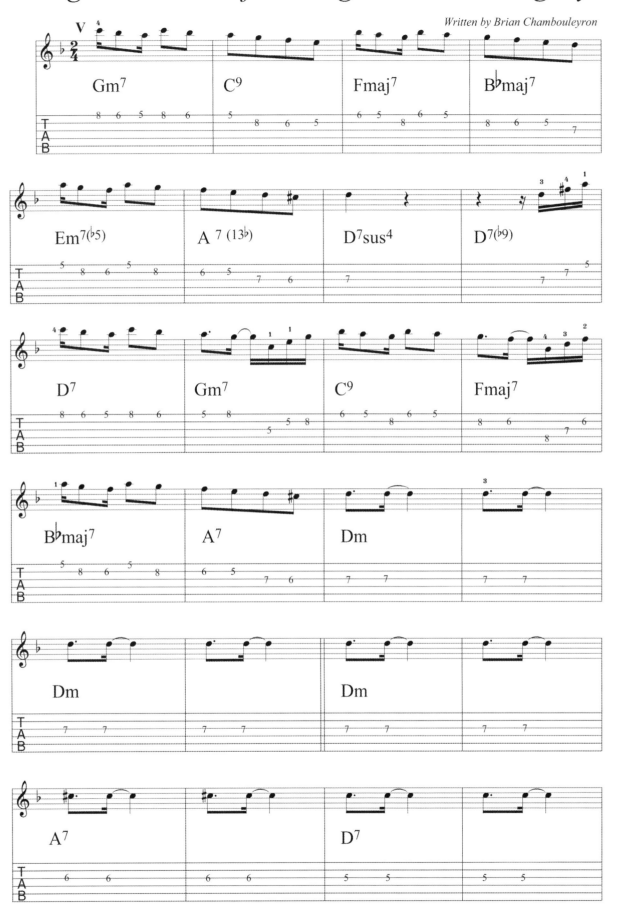

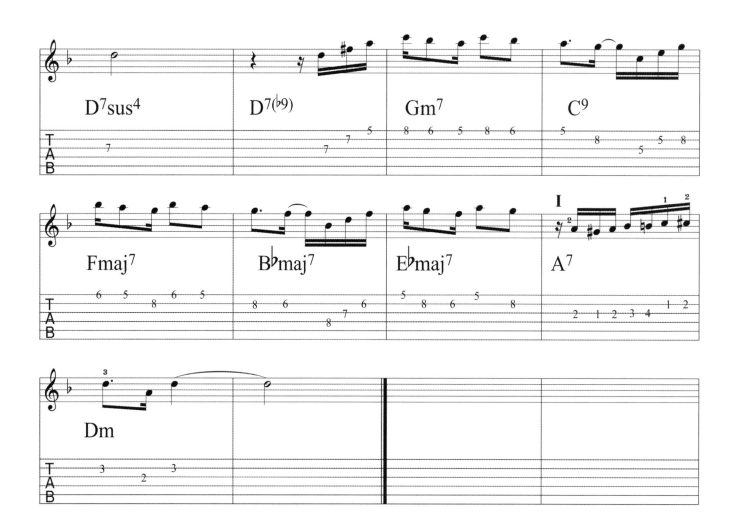

Vals from Perú

Written by Brian Chambouleyron

Guajira from Cuba

Written by Brian Chambouleyron

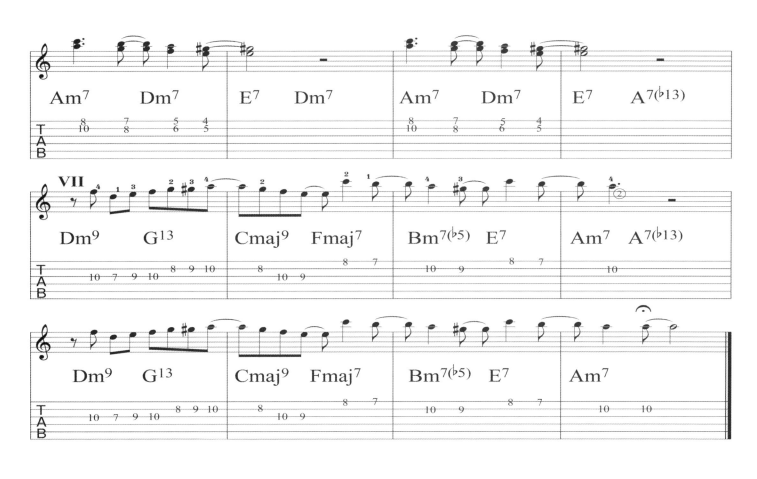

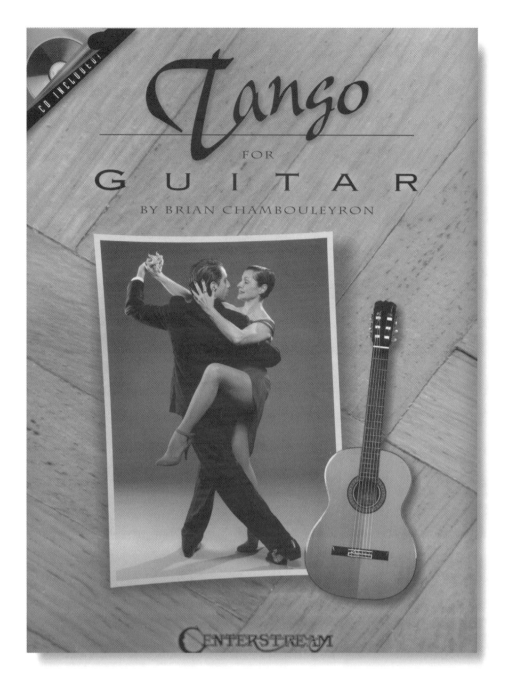

TANGO
FOR GUITAR

By Brian Chambouleyron

At the beginning of the 20th century, the tango was born in Buenos Aires, and it was a style that spread dramatically all over the world. Tango is a dance, a rhythm and a characteristic musical color. The 13 solos in this book were written especially for guitar by award-winning composers Jorge Polanuer and Brian Chambouleyron, and each tune is performed on the CD by Brian, one of the most popular guitarists in Buenos Aires. The solos are presented in different degrees of complexity - tune up with the tuning notes on the CD and play along with the tangos, milangos, waltzes and even a guitar duet. The songs are also repeated on the CD without the lead for you to play the solo part.

00000379 Book/CD Pack .... $ 19.95